CONTENTS

GRANDMA, YOU HAVE A STORY TO SHARE

Grandma

YOU HAVE A STORY TO SHARE

STORIES, MEMORIES AND MOMENTS THAT HAVE SHAPED YOUR LIFE

Grandma, You Have a Story to Share
www.globalselfpublishing.com | Copyright © 2024
ISBN: 978-1-922664-74-7 (Paperback) 978-1-922664-75-4 (Hardback)

GRANDMA
YOU HAVE A STORY TO SHARE

INTRODUCTION

Every grandparent has a story to tell, although many are never provided with the opportunity to share or capture those special memories, moments and stories in one place.

This journal has been carefully designed so grandmothers can share their life stories and provide the answers to many questions that family and friends have never asked.

Grandma, use this journal to share your wonderful life. Your stories, memories, and moments will remain a keepsake for generations to come.

GRANDMA'S INTRODUCTION

A Message From Grandma

Grandma's Introduction

A message before I begin.

FULL NAME

DATE

Family Tree

Great-Grandmother

Great-Grandmother

Great-Grandfather

Great-Grandfather

Grandmother

Grandfather

Mother

Me

Great-Grandmother
Great-Grandmother
Great-Grandfather
Great-Grandfather
Grandmother
Grandfather
Father
My Sibling
My Sibling
My Sibling
My Sibling
My Sibling
My Sibling

SECTION ONE
THE BEGINNING

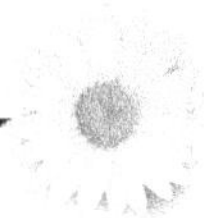

BABY YEARS

Full name at birth____

Date of birth____

Home address when born?_____________________________________

____

Mother's name____

Father's name ____

____

The background to my birth name.

____

____

____

____

____

GRANDMA - YOU HAVE A STORY TO SHARE

My father's age when I was born_____________________________________

Nationality ____

My father's occupation____

My mother's age when I was born______________________________________

Nationality ____

My mother's occupation____

Names and ages of my siblings (if applicable)

____

____

____

Were you in good health as a baby?

____

____

____

Names of uncles and/or aunt's when you were born (as applicable)

____

____

____

____

GRANDMA - YOU HAVE A STORY TO SHARE

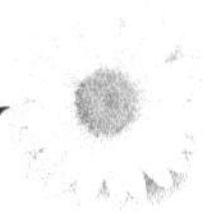

Share with us some information about your parents.

____

____

____

____

____

____

____

____

Grandparent Details

Mothers side.

Grandmother _________________________ Nationality _________________________

Grandfather _________________________ Nationality _________________________

Fathers side

Grandmother _________________________ Nationality _________________________

Grandfather _________________________ Nationality _________________________

GRANDMA - YOU HAVE A STORY TO SHARE

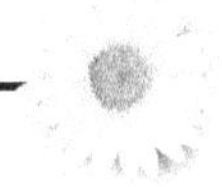

This is something that you may not know about our family history.

GRANDMA - YOU HAVE A STORY TO SHARE

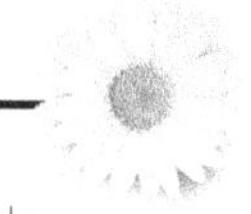

Use these pages to include any photos or further information about your family or baby years.

SECTION TWO
GROWING UP

CHILDHOOD YEARS

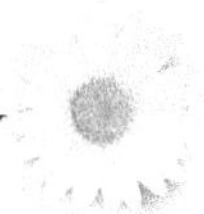

What is your earliest memory as a child?

____

____

____

____

____

Were you told of any funny things or unique characteristics you had as a toddler?

____

____

____

____

____

____

____

GRANDMA - YOU HAVE A STORY TO SHARE

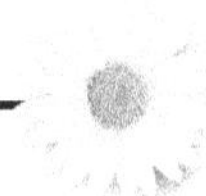

As a toddler, what games or activities did you like to play?

What was your favourite toy growing up?

Did you have a pet or any pets as a young child?

GRANDMA - YOU HAVE A STORY TO SHARE

Did you have a favourite television show you loved to watch as a child?

What was your favourite book or books that you loved as child?

Do you recall being involved in any accidents or hurting yourself as a young child? If so, is there a story behind the accident or injury?

GRANDMA - YOU HAVE A STORY TO SHARE

Was there a moment you recall getting into big trouble as a child?
Was there a punishment?

Was there a special celebration that you recall attending as a child?

GRANDMA - YOU HAVE A STORY TO SHARE

What are your fondest memories between the ages of 5 - 12?

Use these pages to include any childhood photos.

GRANDMA - YOU HAVE A STORY TO SHARE

Use these pages to include any childhood photos.

What was your favourite meal as a child?

Did you have any close friends as a child? If so, please provide some names and details.

Was there a sport or special interest that you started participating in at a young age?

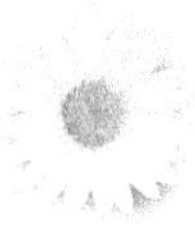

EARLY SCHOOL YEARS

My elementary/primary school was called...

Provide the school location details.

Describe your school. Was it in a city or rural location? Was it large or small? What were some of the backgrounds of the children that attended?

GRANDMA - YOU HAVE A STORY TO SHARE

Was there a teacher that really stood out to you that made an impact on your childhood or education?

Provide details of your most memorable moment or story from your early school years.

GRANDMA - YOU HAVE A STORY TO SHARE

Did you have any close friends at school?

What kind of student were you? Were you well-behaved or mischievous?

GRANDMA - YOU HAVE A STORY TO SHARE

What were your favourite subjects?

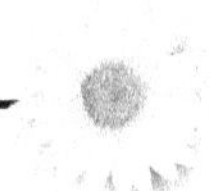

Was there anything that you found challenging or difficult during your early school years?

GRANDMA - YOU HAVE A STORY TO SHARE

Use these pages to include any photos or further notes from your early school years.

 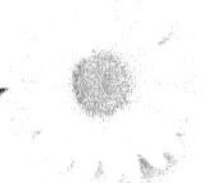

TEENAGE YEARS

Describe what you were like as a teenager.

What were your key interests?

GRANDMA - YOU HAVE A STORY TO SHARE

Did you date anyone in your teenage years? If so, share some details or a story.

Is there anything you regret doing as a teenager?

GRANDMA - YOU HAVE A STORY TO SHARE

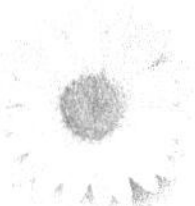

When and where did you learn to drive a vehicle?

At what age did you get your vehicle licence?

What was your first vehicle/mode of transport that you purchased?

Share an experience from your early years of driving.

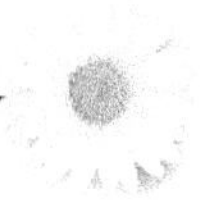

Use this page to include a photo of a vehicle you have owned.

GRANDMA - YOU HAVE A STORY TO SHARE

Was there a particular kind of music that you enjoyed listening to in your teens?

What was a favourite movie from your teens?

What were some of the hobbies or activities that you enjoyed most as a teenager?

GRANDMA - YOU HAVE A STORY TO SHARE

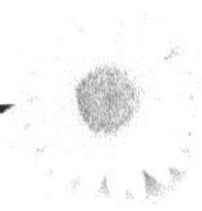

Was there a special holiday destination that you visited? If so, provide some details.

List 3 words that best describe you as a teenager?

1.

2.

3.

GRANDMA - YOU HAVE A STORY TO SHARE

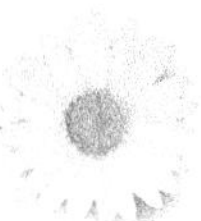

Did you attend High School? If so, where was it located and what was it called?

What subjects did you enjoy at High School?

Did you have a close friendship group? If so, provide some names and details.

GRANDMA - YOU HAVE A STORY TO SHARE

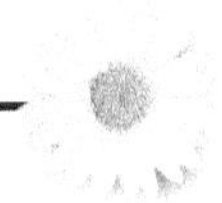

Describe one of your most memorable accomplishments at school.

Did you have a nickname at school?

With what you know now, would you have done anything differently as a teenager?

GRANDMA - YOU HAVE A STORY TO SHARE

Use this page to include any High School photos or extra details.

GRANDMA - YOU HAVE A STORY TO SHARE

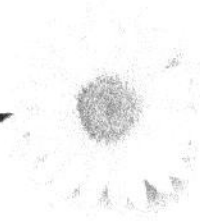

Do you have any other stories, memories or moments from your teenage years that you would like to share?

SECTION THREE
WHEN I WAS..

GRANDMA - YOU HAVE A STORY TO SHARE

When I was a child, I always looked forward to....

When I was a teenager, I always dreamed of becoming...

When I was a teenager, the biggest news story I can recall was...

When I was growing up, my three favourite movies were...

1.

2.

3.

GRANDMA - YOU HAVE A STORY TO SHARE

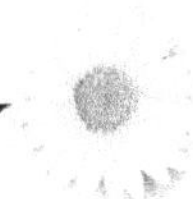

When I completed school, the year was...

When I turned 21 yrs, I celebrated by....

When I was in my teens, the silliest thing I did was.....

When I was in my teens, I had a celebrity crush on....

When I was growing up, my three favourite bands were..

1.

2.

3.

GRANDMA - YOU HAVE A STORY TO SHARE

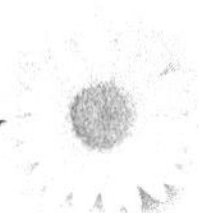

When I was young, I regret not...

When I was a teenager, I earned some money by....

When I left home for the first time, I went and lived....

GRANDMA - YOU HAVE A STORY TO SHARE

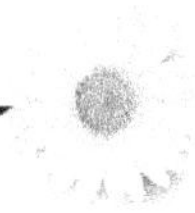

These are the lessons I learnt as a teenager that I wish to pass onto my children and grandchildren.

SECTION FOUR
PARENTHOOD

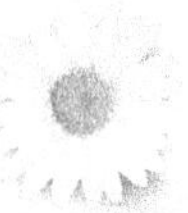

BECOMING A PARENT

My age when I first became a parent________________________

Where were you living when you became a first time mother?

Explain how you felt emotionally when you became a parent?

Was there anything that you were under-prepared for?

GRANDMA - YOU HAVE A STORY TO SHARE

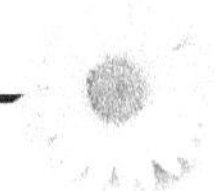

My employment when I had my first child (if applicable)

If you have other children, list the locations and dates they were born.

Name	Location	D.O.B

How many children had you planned to have?

GRANDMA - YOU HAVE A STORY TO SHARE

What has been your biggest challenge as a parent?

What **3 key responsibilities** do you believe are important as a parent?

1.

2.

3.

GRANDMA - YOU HAVE A STORY TO SHARE

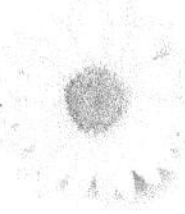

BECOMING A GRANDPARENT

What year did you first become a grandparent?

What was the name of your first grandchild?

If you have more than one grandchild, list their names below.

Share a special memory of when you first became a grandparent.

GRANDMA - YOU HAVE A STORY TO SHARE

Do you have a grandparent nickname?

What do you enjoy most about being a grandparent?

What advice would you give to your grandchild/grandchildren?

Use these pages to include some parenting or grandparenting photos

Use these pages to include some parenting or grandparenting photos

GRANDMA - YOU HAVE A STORY TO SHARE

Use this page to share some more parenting or grandparenting stories or information and a family photo below

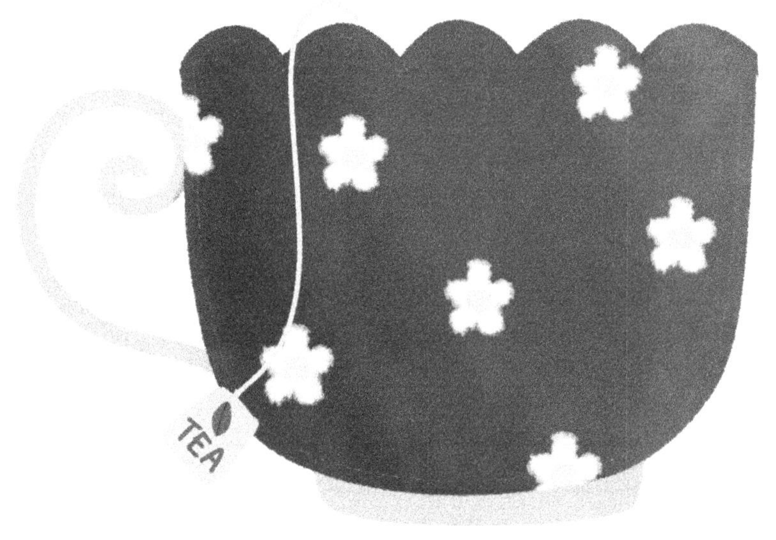

TEA

SECTION FIVE
LIFE, TRAVEL AND ADVENTURE

GRANDMA - YOU HAVE A STORY TO SHARE

If I could travel anywhere in the world for a holiday, I would visit..

I would choose this location because..

The activity or hobby that I enjoy most to participate now in is..

You could call it my 'super-power', but I have the unique ability to be able to....

GRANDMA - YOU HAVE A STORY TO SHARE

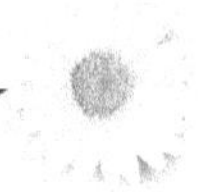

My biggest fear is....

If I could invite 3 famous people to dinner (deceased or alive), they would be...

1.

2.

3.

If you could re-live and experience a personal moment in your life again, it would be?

GRANDMA - YOU HAVE A STORY TO SHARE

Not many people would know this about me, so let me share it with you.

If I could re-live and experience a moment in history (a world event), it would be..

GRANDMA - YOU HAVE A STORY TO SHARE

My favourite quote of all time is.

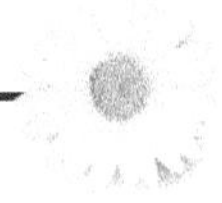

I would recommend that everyone should read...

____

One day in the future, I would like to be best remembered for...

____

____

____

____

____

____

____

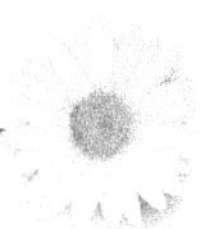

In no particular order, these are some of my proudest moments.

GRANDMA - YOU HAVE A STORY TO SHARE

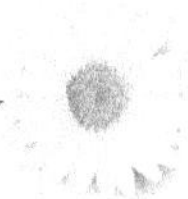

From my 20's, these are some of the jobs that I've had.
(Include the years if they can be recalled)

YEAR   EMPLOYMENT

GRANDMA - YOU HAVE A STORY TO SHARE

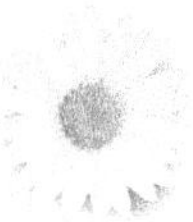

If I could have done anything as a job, it would have been..

The most interesting place I have ever visited has been..

EXPLORE

GRANDMA - YOU HAVE A STORY TO SHARE

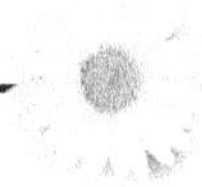

I feel the best way I can help others is by..

If someone was to write a book about my life, the title of the book would be..

I feel happiest when..

GRANDMA - YOU HAVE A STORY TO SHARE

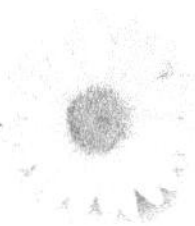

If I had to choose another country to live in, it would be...

because...

These are 3 things that I would like to do over the next 12 months.

GRANDMA - YOU HAVE A STORY TO SHARE

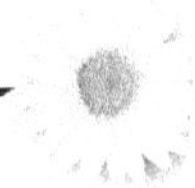

Add any additional notes or information here..

SECTION SIX

MEMORIES AND STORIES

GRANDMA - YOU HAVE A STORY TO SHARE

The best family holiday I've experienced has been..

One of the hardest life experiences I've had to deal with was...

GRANDMA - YOU HAVE A STORY TO SHARE

A great roadtrip I once experienced was...

I had the best meal here and I will never forget it. In fact, I would highly recommend it!

SECTION SEVEN
MY FINAL WORDS

GRANDMA - YOU HAVE A STORY TO SHARE

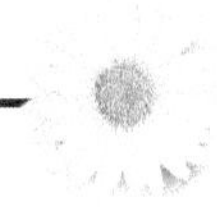

Please include any further information, stories or moments that
have not been shared throughout this journal.

GRANDMA - YOU HAVE A STORY TO SHARE

GRANDMA - YOU HAVE A STORY TO SHARE

GRANDMA - YOU HAVE A STORY TO SHARE

Please include additional photos, letters, postcards or other memorabilia in the pages provided.

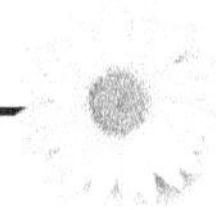

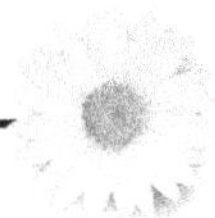

ABOUT THE AUTHOR

Romney Nelson is a Best-Selling author and Founder of Global Self-Publishing, where he is committed to providing the highest quality books to his customers across the globe.

www.globalselfpublishing.com

Also in the Series

Available for purchase via

www.globalselfpublishing.com/storytoshare

and all major online bookstores

Everyone Has a Story to Share

9 781922 664747